Anonymous

Visitor's Guide to Richmond and Vicinity

Embracing a sketch of the city, social statistics and notices of all places in

and about the city of interest to the tourist

Anonymous

Visitor's Guide to Richmond and Vicinity
*Embracing a sketch of the city, social statistics and notices of all places in and about
the city of interest to the tourist*

ISBN/EAN: 9783337193348

Printed in Europe, USA, Canada, Australia, Japan

Cover: Foto ©Andreas Hilbeck / pixelio.de

More available books at **www.hansebooks.com**

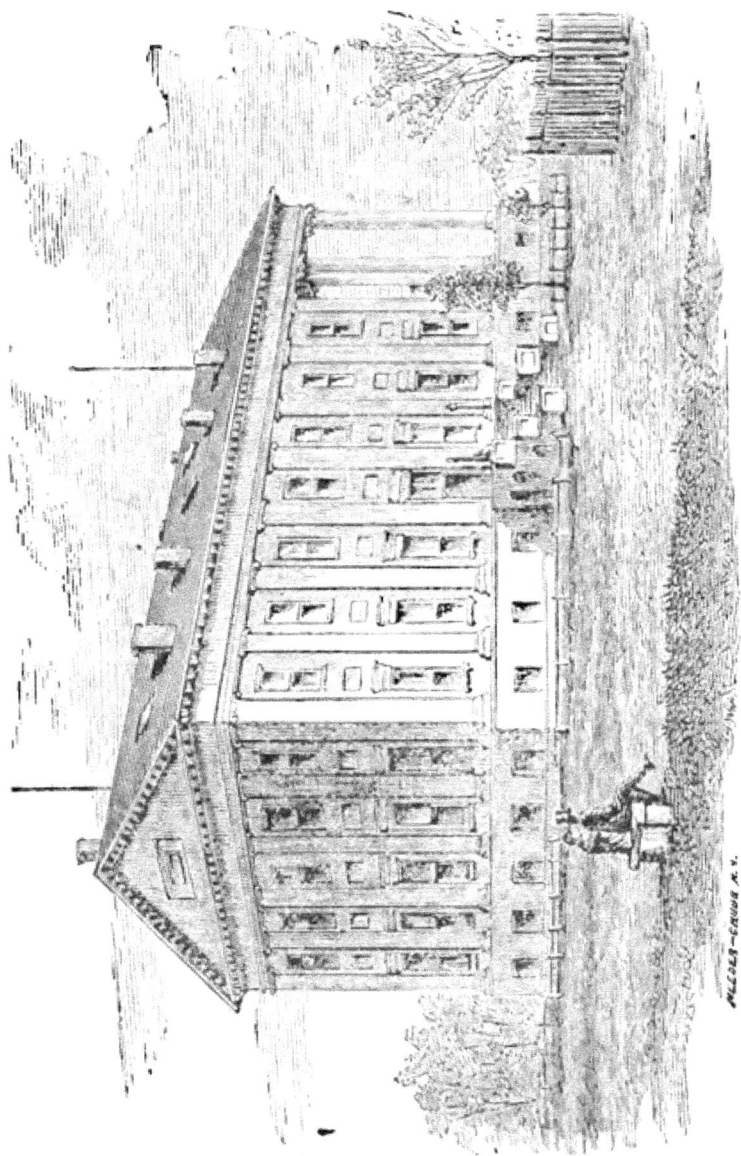

CAPITOL.

[From "Walks about Richmond."]

VISITOR'S GUIDE

TO

RICHMOND

AND VICINITY;

EMBRACING A SKETCH OF THE CITY, SOCIAL STATIS-
TICS AND NOTICES OF ALL PLACES IN AND ABOUT
THE CITY OF INTEREST TO THE TOURIST,

WITH AN

Accurate Map,

AND VIEWS OF THE CAPITOL, WASHINGTON MONUMENT,
LIBBY PRISON AND ST. JOHN'S CHURCH.

Richmond, Va.:

BENJ. BATES, BOOKSELLER AND STATIONER, 1005 MAIN STREET.

1871.

PREFATORY NOTE.

No city in the country as large as Richmond can afford to be without a guide-book for visitors, and it is strange that Richmond, than which there is no place with more historic memories in America, should have been so long lacking in this respect. This work is intended to convey the information needed by tourists—and which should be in the minds of every citizen—in the most simple style and convenient form. We need not add that it makes no pretensions to literary merit.

Table of Contents.

VISITOR'S GUIDE.

RICHMOND.

RICHMOND is the seat of justice of Henrico county, and the capital of Virginia. It is located on the northeast bank of the James River, at the lower falls, and at the head of tide-water. The distance from Richmond to Washington, in an air-line, is one hundred miles. By railroad, it is one hundred and thirty miles from Washington, and one hundred and sixty-eight from Baltimore. The latitude of the capital is 37° 32' 17" north, and the longitude is 77° 27' 28" west.

The city is built on several hills, the most considerable of which are Shockoe and Church Hills, which are separated from each other by Shockoe Creek. It is laid out with a good degree of regularity, in rectangular blocks. The streets running East and West were originally named after the letters of the alphabet, A being nearest the river. They have lost their names, however, and the principal ones are now known as Cary, Main, Franklin, Grace, Broad, Marshall, Clay and Leigh. Most of the streets running North and South are named from the ordinal numbers—First, Second, Third, and so on to Thirty-first. The principal thoroughfares of business are Main, Broad and Cary streets, which are parallel with the river.

EARLY HISTORY.

A VILLAGE on the James River, near the part of Richmond now called Rocketts, is more than once

mentioned in the early records of the Old Dominion.
A settlement was made at the falls of the river by
Master West, with a colony of one hundred and
twenty people driven from Jamestown by famine in
1609. In 1644-'45, the Assembly of Virginia ordered
a fort to be erected at the Falls of James River,
to be called "Forte Charles." In 1679, certain
privileges were granted to Col. Byrd upon the con-
dition that he should settle fifty able-bodied and
well-armed men near the Falls as a protection to
the frontier against the Indians." But Richmond was
not made a town by legislative enactment until during
the reign of George III. This was done in May, 1742,
and the town was to be located on the land of Col. Wm.
Byrd.

Thirty-five years later, (in the year 1777,) the troops,
arms, ammunition and public records of the State
were removed hither from the Capitol at Williamsburg, in view of the exposed position of that town.
And, from the same cause, no less than because
of the tendency of the population to go westward, an
act was passed in May, 1779, removing the seat of Government also to the same place. At this time (says
Howe's Historical Collections) Richmond was but an in-
significant place, scarcely affording sufficient accommodations for the officers of Government. The Legislature
bestowed upon it the title of a city ; but it was only such
in embryo, possessing few objects of interest, except
grand natural scenery. The analogy of the situation, it is
said, to Richmond-on-the-Thames, in England, sug-
gested the name of the town. In 1781, Richmond
was invaded by Benedict Arnold, at the head of
a British army—one of the boldest acts of the Revo-

lution. He burned some public and private buildings, and a large quantity of tobacco. The Governor of the State fled to Manchester.

POPULATION.

TEN YEARS after it was made the capital Richmond
had three hundred houses. The population of the city
was, in 1800, five thousand seven hundred and thirty-
seven; in 1810, nine thousand seven hundred and
eighty-five; in 1820, twelve thousand six hundred and
seven; in 1830, sixteen thousand and sixty; in 1840,
twenty thousand one hundred and fifty-three; in
1850, twenty-seven thousand five hundred and fifty;
in 1860, thirty-seven thousand nine hundred and ten;
in 1870, fifty-one thousand.

SCHOOLS AND COLLEGES.

ACCORDING to the census of 1870, there are three col-
leges in Richmond, with seven male teachers and one
hundred and sixty male pupils, and an annual income
of about $14,000; one Medical College, with nineteen
male teachers and one hundred and forty-five male
pupils; and one Commercial College, with two male
teachers and one hundred and forty pupils. There are
also fifty-six Private Schools, for day scholars, with
eighty-six teachers and two thousand and ninety two
pupils; and about ten large Boarding Schools, from
which we have no correct official returns. There are
forty-three Sabbath Schools, in which nine thousand
nine hundred and sixty-seven children are taught.

The Public School system is conducted after the
most approved models. It is controlled by a Board of
Education, of which the Mayor is *ex-officio* President.
Mr. Jas. H. Binford is the Superintendent, and his

office is in the Central School Building, corner of 12th
and Clay streets. On the 1st of January, 1871, there
were in the city thirty-nine white and thirty-three colored schools, with sixty-one white and twelve colored
teachers. A Teachers' Institute is in operation, with
most gratifying results.

Besides the above educational institutions there is a
Normal School for colored persons, with seven teachers
and one hundred and twenty pupils, and an income of
$7,300; and there is also a High School with two teach-
ers, forty-five pupils, and an income of $500.

LIBRARIES.

RICHMOND has a State library of twenty thousand
volumes, and one college library of eight thousand
volumes. There are also sixteen thousand volumes in
church libraries, six thousand five hundred and fifty-
eight in sabbath school libraries, and thirty-eight thousand two hundred and twenty-five in private libraries.
These figures are taken from the census of 1870, but
so far as private libraries are concerned, fall far short of
the actual number of volumes.

THE CAPITOL.

IN THE very heart of the city, and on a commmanding
eminence, stands the Virginia State Capitol. It is a
stuccoed brick building, and is an imperfect copy of
one of the most graceful and grand structures ever con-
ceived—the *Maison Carree* of Nismes, France, and
was selected by Thomas Jefferson. The building
was finished in 1792. Men recently deceased told
of the time when it was unstuccoed, and presented
altogether a very ugly appearance. The Capitol Square
was then "a rugged piece of ground, cut up by gullies

and covered with a wild growth of Jamestown weeds and chinquepin bushes."* On each side of the Capitol was a long horse rack, and in front of the portico stood an unpainted wooden belfry. The portico was then reached by a narrow winding stone stairway, now closed, which gave to the goats and kids which sported about the grounds a convenient access to the portico, where they found shelter in hot weather.

THE BASEMENT. In the basement of the Capitol, at this day, are the offices of the First and Second Auditors, the Treasurer of the State, Register of the Land Office, and the rooms occupied by the apparatus for heating the building. Ascending to the second floor we reach the rotunda.

Here the principal object of interest to strangers is the fine STATUE OF WASHINGTON by the French Sculptor, Houdon. It was made at Paris, by order of the Virginia Assembly, under the direction of Jefferson, shortly after the close of the Revolution of 1776. The costume of the figure is the military dress of the Revolution. One hand holds a cane, the other rests upon fasces, with which are united the sword and plow share, and over all hangs a martial cloak. The inscription on the pedestal was written by James Madison. It is as follows:

GEORGE WASHINGTON.

The General Assembly of the Commonwealth of Virginia have caused this statue to be erected as a monument of affection and gratitude to George Washington; who, uniting to the endowments of the HERO the virtues of the patriot, and exerting both in establishing the liberties of his country, has rendered his name dear to his fellow-citizens, and has given the world an immortal example of true glory. Done in the year of Christ, one thousand seven hundred and eighty-eight, and in the year of the Commonwealth the twelfth.

RICHMOND IN BYE GONE DAYS, by an Old Citizen, published by George M. West, 1856.

From the rotunda the visitor passes on the one side to the Hall of the House of Delegates, and on the other, to the Chamber of the Senate. The most notable object in the Senate Chamber is the full-length portrait of Gen. Robert E. Lee, painted by John A. Elder, a distinguished Virginia artist, and now the property of the State. It is considered an excellent picture.

HALL OF THE HOUSE OF DELEGATES.—THE lower branch of the Virginia Legislature here meets. In the same room the Constitutional Conventions of 1829-'30, 1850 and 1867, and the Secession Convention of 1861, held their sessions. That of 1867, known as the Reconstruction Convention, was the first body assembled under the authority of the State, or National Government, in Virginia, in which colored men held seats as members. The President of the first Constitutional Convention was James Madison ; of the second, John Y. Mason ; and of the third, John C. Underwood. The Secession Convention was presided over by John Janney.

Here is to be seen the Speakers' chair of the Colonial House of Burgesses, originally decorated with the Royal arms of Great Britain, which, having been removed from Williamsburg, the former site of the Capitol of the State, to Richmond, is now occupied by the Speaker of the House of Delegates. This chair was crushed by the falling floor of the Court of Appeals room, but its fragments were gathered up, and have been put together by the Superintendent of Public Buildings in their present form. The walls of the room were formerly adorned with full-length portraits of Earl Chatham and Thos. Jefferson.

SENATE CHAMBER.—This room, in which the State Senate now meets, was, during several years of the war, occupied as the Hall of the House of Representatives of the Confederate States. The Speaker's chair was then on the south side of the chamber.

STATE LIBRARY.—Immediately above the Senate Chamber is the State Library, which, although deficient, perhaps, in its supply of recent publications, has a store of volumes pertaining to the early history of the country second to few libraries of the kind in the Union.

ON THE SAME FLOOR we find what was once the Court of Appeals room, and the offices now occupied by the Adjutant General, the Governor and his Secretary, the Superintendents of Public Instruction and Printing, and the Secretary of the Commonwealth. There can be no more appropriate place than this to call the reader's attention to the terrible calamity which occurred on this spot April 26th, 1870, and known throughout Virginia as

THE CAPITOL DISASTER.—The room of the Court of Appeals was the scene of this horrible occurrence. On the 16th day of March, a new City Council, appointed by Gov. Walker, in pursuance of the " Enabling Act," elected H. K. Ellyson Mayor of Richmond. The constitutionality of said act was contested by the incumbent of the mayoralty, Geo. Chahoon, and ultimately the question was brought before the Supreme Court of Appeals. The case had been argued, and the Court had announced that its decision would be rendered on Wednesday, April 27th. On that day, an immense concourse of persons, including members of the Legislature, lawyers, representatives of the press, policemen, visitors from various parts of the

State, and representatives of almost every class in the community, gathered in this small room to hear the result. Two of the five Judges had taken their seats, the clerk was ready to read the orders, and the dense crowd waited in perfect silence the opening of the Court. Suddenly there was a crash, and those in the gallery saw the floor of the crowded room beneath them quiver. A moment later, and the floor gave way with another awful crash, and the clerk's office, court-room and gallery, with their whole human freight of four hundred persons, were precipitated a distance of about forty feet to the room below, falling together with a mass of bricks, mortar, splinters, beams, iron bars, desks and chairs; and then, upon all this, in a second more, the false ceiling, with its supports, came tumbling down, burying the victims beneath its immense weight. The atmosphere was thick with a dense cloud of dust, and the human beings sent up a groan which will ring forever in the ears of those who heard it. In a moment a few survivors clinging to the windows and fragments of hanging timber, and the bare and torn walls, were all that remained to mark the place where just before there was a scene of life, vigor and hope. Sixty-two persons were killed, and two hundred and forty-nine were wounded. Among the former, were Patrick Henry Aylett, N. P. Howard and Powhatan Roberts, distinguished members of the Virginia Bar, Dr. J. B. Brock, city editor of the *Enquirer* newspaper, J. W. D. Bland, a talented colored member of the State Senate, Captain Charters, Chief Engineer of the Fire Department, E. M. Schofield, City Assessor, and many other persons prominent in the city or State. The list of wounded contained also a mournful array of leading citizens. By this disaster, Richmond sustained, perhaps, the greatest of the many calamities she has been called upon to suffer since the civil war, and the city will not for years recover from the shock.

THE WASHINGTON MONUMENT.

This work of Art, is an object of great interest to all visitors to the Capital of Virginia. It was erected in accordance with an Act of Assembly passed February 22d, 1849, by which commissioners were appointed to superintend the work. The commissioners offered a premium of $500 for the best plan or design of the monument, and on the 8th of January, 1850, the model submitted by Thomas Crawford, of Rome, was selected. The ceremony of laying the corner stone took place on the 22d of February, 1850. Zachary Taylor, President of the United States, and other prominent dignitaries were present by invitation of the Legislature. On the 27th of June, articles of agreement were entered into with Crawford, whereby it was stipulated that the equestrian group in bronze should be fifteen English feet from the upper surface of the platform to the top of the chapeau, and that the pedestrian statues should be ten English feet in height. At first Jefferson, Henry, Marshall, Morgan, General Harry Lee and an allegorical figure of Virginia, were selected for the pedestrian statues; but afterwards, Andrew Lewis was substituted for Morgan, George Mason for General Lee, and Thomas Nelson for the allegorical figure. On the 10th of October, 1857, Crawford died, at London, after completing models of all the statuary, except Lewis and Nelson and the "trophies." The commissioners contracted with Randolph Rogers of New York, for the completion of the work, and the statues were cast at the Royal Foundry, Munich.

The equestrian group arrived in Richmond in November, 1857, and was hauled to the Square by the citizens on the 24th. It was erected with the statues of Henry and Jefferson, and unveiled on the next succeeding 22d of February with appropriate ceremonies. The statue of Mason was received and erected early in 1860, and the war coming on soon after, the monument remained in *statu quo* until 1867, when the statues of Marshall, Lewis and Nelson were received. The allegorical figures were all received in 1868, and with their erection the monument was completed.

The following shows the disposition of the statuary and the inscriptions on the shields of the allegorical figures :

Finance,	- opposite	Nelson,	} Yorktown, } Saratoga.
Colonial Times,	"	Lewis,	} Point Pleasant, } Valley Forge.
Justice,	- - "	Marshall,	} Great Bridge. } Stony Point.
Revolution,	- "	Henry,	} Eutaw Springs, } Trenton.
Independence.	"	Jefferson,	} King's Mountain, } Princeton.
Bill of Rights,	"	Mason,	} Guildford C. H., } Bunker Hill.

By an interesting " Historical account of the Washington Monument," (published by Wm. A. R. Nye, Richmond,) from which the materials for this sketch are derived, we learn that the total cost of the monument was $259,913.26. The total amount realized from donations and the interest thereon was $47,212 67.

WASHINGTON MONUMENT.
[From "Walks about Richmond."]

THE GOVERNOR'S HOUSE,

Or Executive Mansion, as it is called, is an unpretending building on the north-east corner of the Capitol Grounds. The Governor's House preceding the present one was a very plain wooden building of two stories, with only two small rooms on the first floor. A historian says it was for many years destitute of paint, and the furniture was in keeping with the Republican simplicity of the edifice and of its occupants, from Henry and Jefferson down to Monroe and Page. The palings around the yard were usually dilapidated, and the goats that sported on the steep hill sides of the Capitol Square, claimed and exercised the privilege of grazing on His Excellency's grounds.

GUARD HOUSE.

The building on the Capitol Square, near the Ninth street gate, was for many years occupied as Barracks for the Public or State Guard. It is now merely a bell-tower, the hours being struck by means of an electric wire connecting with Police Headquarters.

ST. PAUL'S EPISCOPAL CHURCH

Is somewhat noted as the most frequented by the fashionable people in Richmond during the war. Here Jefferson Davis and Gen. Robert E. Lee had pews, and the former was a regular attendant upon divine service. On the memorable 2d of April, 1865, Mr. Davis was seated in his pew, when the sexton handed him a telegram from Gen. Lee, conveying the information that Petersburg was lost to the Confederates, and Richmond must be evacuated. That night the evacuation took place, and on the next day the Union troops entered the city.

The church is located on the corner of Ninth and Grace streets, immediately opposite the western gate of the Capitol Square, and within a few blocks of either of the leading hotels. Rev. Chas. Minnegerode, D. D., who was Rector during the war. and who is a warm personal friend of Mr. Davis, still occupies the pulpit.

THE LEE HOUSE,

NEAR St. Paul's, and within two blocks of the site of the Spotswood Hotel, is the house occupied as a residence by Gen. Robert E. Lee, while General-in-Chief of the Confederate armies. It is a plain brick building, on Franklin street, (No. 707,) between 7th and 8th, now occupied by Mrs. Geo. Davis.

THE CUSTOM HOUSE.

THIS is a large granite building, fronting on Main street between 10th and 11th, and extending back to Bank street. It was occupied during the war by the Treasury Department of the Confederate States, and President Davis had his office in the third story.

At present. the first floor is used as the Post Office, and on the second floor are the offices of the Collector of Customs, Collector, Assessor and Supervisor of Internal Revenue, and United States District Attorney. On the third floor are the United States Court-room and the offices of the Judges, Marshal and Clerks. The fourth floor is taken up with jury rooms. This building passed through the great fire of evacuation night without injury, while all other houses on both sides of Main street, between 9th and 13th, were either partially or totally destroyed.

THEATRE.

THE RICHMOND OPERA HOUSE stands on the corner of Broad and 7th streets. It is a building of no pretensions to architectural beauty, but is the only place of amusement in the city regularly open for dramatic performances.

THE JEFF. DAVIS MANSION.

AT the south-west corner of Marshall and 11th streets, and on a very commanding height, now known as President Hill, stands a large rectangular three-storied stuccoed building, built many years ago by Judge Thos. W. Brockenbrough, a gentleman of large means, as a private residence. The grounds attached to the house were laid out in the most beautiful style, and were adorned with statuary and numerous fountains.

When the Seat of War of the Confederate Government was removed from Montgomery to Richmond, the City Council purchased this property, with a view to presenting it to Jefferson Davis, then recently elected President of the Confederate States. When Mr. Davis arrived here, the tender of the property was formally made to him, but he respectfully, though firmly, refused the present. The city, however, declined to take it back or cancel the purchase, and Mr. Davis finally agreed to occupy it, free of rent, with the express understanding that it was to remain the property of the city. This he did until the evacuation of the city, in 1865. When the Federal troops entered the city, they took possession of it, and it was occupied either as a residence, or as headquarters, by each of the Military Commanders who ruled Virginia, until the army was finally withdrawn from the State, in 1870. The property was then restored to the city, whose authorities have remodelled it for school purposes.

It was from the rear porch of this dwelling that little Joe Davis, son of Jefferson Davis, met his death, by falling to the pavement below.

MONUMENTAL CHURCH.

THE MONUMENTAL EPISCOPAL CHURCH, a handsome octagonal edifice on Broad street, between 12th and 13th, is erected upon the spot where perished, in 1811, sixty persons, or more, by the burning of the Richmond Theatre. When the fire by which the theatre was burned broke out, there were not less than six hundred persons in the house, and the play for the evening was just about drawing to a close. The scenery first caught fire, and the flames spreading with fearful rapidity, the house was soon but a heap of ashes. Among those who lost their lives, were Geo. W. Smith, Governor of the State, A. B. Venable, President of the Bank, and many ladies and gentlemen of old Virginia families. The remains of the unfortunate victims of the sad catastrophe are deposited in a marble urn which stands in the front portico of the church.

MEDICAL COLLEGE OF VIRGINIA.

THIS Institution is located on the corner of College and Marshall streets. It was established in 1838, as a department of the Hampden Sidney College. The building is a fine specimen of the Egyptian style of architecture. Adjoining the College is the Richmond Infirmary under the superintendence of Dr. Horace D. Taliaferro.

ST. JOHN'S CHURCH.

This building occupies the block on Church Hill, bounded by Broad, Grace, Twenty-fourth and Twenty-fifth streets. It is the oldest place of worship in Richmond, but this is its least claim upon the veneration of the visitor. Surrounded by an antiquated brick wall, in the midst of a church yard full of tombstones, and embowered by umbrageous trees, it presents a most picturesque appearance. It was here that Patrick Henry, in the Virginia Convention of 1775, raised his eloquent voice for the freedom of the colonies and uttered the ever memorable words, *"give me liberty or give me death."* Among the other members of this Convention were Madison, Marshall, Monroe, Pendleton, Wythe, Nicholas, Greyson, George Mason, Edmund Randolph and Innis.

THE OLD STONE HOUSE,

Is on the north side of Main, between Nineteenth and Twentieth streets. It is the oldest dwelling house in Richmond and was among the first ever built here. The builder and first owner was Jacob Ege, a German immigrant, in whose family the ownership remained for six generations. President Monroe, when a young man attending school, boarded here, and at that time it was considered a fine house. It has been honored by visits from Presidents Washington, Jefferson and Madison, General Lafayette and Patrick Henry, and tradition has it that it was for a time General Washington's Headquarters during the Revolution of 1776–'81.

STATE COURT HOUSE.

The building now known by this name is on Eleventh

street, between Marshall and Broad. It was built as a place of worship for the use of the congregation of "Disciples of Christ," and was occupied by them until the summer of 1870, when it became necessary for the House of Delegates to provide another place of meeting, in view of the Capitol Disaster. They then bought this church and occupied it for several months; after which it was neatly fitted up as a State Court House. It is now occupied in part as a place of meeting for the Court of Appeals, and in part as a law library. The old State Court House was located on the Capitol Square, near the east gate. It was burned in April, 1865, and the grass is now green where it stood, not one stone remaining.

THE MILITARY PRISONS

OF Richmond are nearly always first inquired for by tourists from the North, as well as by not a few from the South. These prisons were four in number, and all have become familiar by name to the people of the United States. The first house used in this city as a place of confinement for Federal soldiers captured in battle, was on Main street near Twenty-fifth, where were placed the prisoners from Big Bethel. But the large number brought hither after the first battle of Manassas made it necessary to provide quarters more commodious and secure.

THE LIBBY was then selected. This is a two-story brick building, located on the corner of Cary and Twentieth streets. It was built for a ship chandlery, and was used as such several years previous to the war by Mr. L. Libby, from whom it takes its name. Here were confined thousands of Union soldiers between

July 1861, and April 1865, and it was frequently crowded to overflowing, some spending many months within its walls, and many being kept here only a few days, until it was found convenient to take them further south—to Salisbury, or Andersonville. All over the walls may still be seen the names of prisoners scratched there during their confinement, and relic hunters have chipped some of the bricks until they are as rough as millstones. Attempts at escape were of course numerous, but they were rarely successful. The most noted was that of Colonel Streight, who, with no tools but forks, tunnelled under the street from the basement of the prison to a vacant lot about twenty feet distant, and with about sixty comrades got away under the cover of the darkness of a stormy night. They were hidden in the city for two or three days by resident unionists, and most of them after many remarkable adventures made their way north. The Libby is now used as a sumac factory and bone mill.

CASTLE THUNDER—On Cary street, between Eighteenth and Nineteenth, only one square from the Libby, is also still standing, and is now used, as before the war, as a tobacco factory. In Confederate times it was the place in which citizens of doubtful loyalty to the Confederacy were locked up, together with spies and deserters. One or more executions took place within its walls. A large black dog, by some called a mastiff and by others a blood-hound, was a member of the guard of the Castle and a terror to its inmates. It was reported among the negroes that he subsisted on human flesh.

CASTLE LIGHTNING—On Lumpkin's Alley, formerly a negro prison, was, during the first year of the war, a place of confinement for political or State pris-

B

oners.   It is memorable as the house in which the Hon.
John Minor Botts, Burnham Wardwell, and other Virginia Unionists were incarcerated,   The presiding
genius of this establishment was Capt. Alexander, who
afterwards took charge of Castle Thunder.

BELLE ISLE is an island of the James River, just
above the Petersburg Railroad Bridge, and best seen
from Gamble's Hill, It is now occupied almost entirely
by the works of the Old Dominion Nail Company, and
the houses of its operatives.   It was, probably, the
largest prison camp for Federal soldiers in Virginia.
The prisoners were all kept in tents on the plain, and
were guarded by a company of infantry and a battery
of artillery placed on the heights in rear of, and fully
commanding, the camp.   There was no escape, except
by swimming a rapid and dangerous current, even if
the guard was eluded.   A large number of prisoners
attempted to get away one night in 1862.   Several were
shot, some were drowned, and all, or nearly all, the
rest were recaptured.

THE SOLDIERS' HOME, a large tobacco factory on
the corner of Cary and 7th streets, was used as a kind
of Home of Relay for soldiers on their way to the
army, and for the detention of stragglers and citizens
without passes.   It was always crowded, and was by no
means a pleasant place to spend the night.   Lieut.
Benj. Bates was the officer in charge.

HOSPITALS FOR CONFEDERATE SOLDIERS.

MANY a wounded and maimed soldier of the South
remembers, with grateful emotions, the hospitals of
this city, and will always bless the ladies, to whose
attentions and unremitting care and watchfulness he

owes his life. The first hospitals were prepared at a moment's notice, and, of course, were not well adapted to the purpose. They were mainly unoccupied tobacco factories, and they were generally abandoned as buildings more suitable were leased or erected. The first building of any note, or of capacity sufficient to merit the name of an army hospital, used as such, was the

St. Charles Hotel, on the corner of Main and 15th streets. Here were brought the sick from Beauregard's army, and those wounded at the first battle of Manassas. The private residence of Judge John Robertson, at the upper end of Main street, was used as an officers' hospital, and was supported by two maiden ladies of this city. The hospital of

St. Francis de Sales, established on Brook Avenue near Bacon's Quarter Branch, was also used as a receptacle for sick soldiers. As battles became more frequent, it became necessary to provide additional quarters for the wounded. The hospitals were full; many citizens had taken the soldiers into their houses, and no room was left. A large tobacco warehouse, occupying the greater part of the square between Grace and Broad, and 17th and 18th streets, was emptied of the tobacco, and temporary beds and bunks erected there. This was the famous Seabrook's Hospital.

Later, large wooden houses were erected at Howard's Grove, a cool and shady spot one mile east of the city, on the Mechanicsville Turnpike. Here were accommodations for several thousand persons, and it continued full until the close of the war. But the most noted, as it was the largest of all, was

Chimborazo.—This hospital comprised a series of one story wooden houses, built on Chimborazo Heights.

in the southeastern suburbs of the city. Here were to be found soldiers from every Southern State, and from hence many a poor fellow was taken to the neighboring cemetery of Oakwood, where all the dead from this hospital were buried. Several of the Southern States also had separate and distinct hospitals here, in which many of the soldiers of those States, respectively, were cared for, at the expense of the State.

NEGRO JAILS AND AUCTION HOUSES.

In the days of slavery, jails were built in which negroes for sale and hire were kept and boarded at a *per diem*, and halls were fitted up, in which they were exhibited whenever possible purchasers came 'round. Soon these jails were insufficient to accommodate all the business, and sellers wishing to take better advantage of the competition among buyers, many of whom came from the far south, yearly, to increase or replenish their labor, opened auction houses. In these the slaves were arranged in rows, on benches, around the room, awaiting their turn to be called to the auctioneer's block.

These auction houses were all situated on Franklin, near the corner of Wall street, and it was thought necessary that the jails should be in close proximity, so that the slaves could be more readily taken to the auction houses, and with less danger of escapes; and, also, that purchasers who were making up their lots might board near the jails, (the leading hotels being on Franklin street,) until they could buy their supplies.

The jails were, therefore, almost without exception, in the bottom between Franklin and Broad streets, on jail alley. The most noted of these because the largest, and, therefore, able to accommodate the largest number, was the one known as

LUMPKIN'S.—This house was built some time about the year 1825, by Bacon Tait, for this purpose, and was used as such until the close of the war. During the war, a portion of it was used in connection with Castle Lightning as a temporary receptacle for political prisoners. After the war, it was ntted up by the Rev. Dr. Colver, a Baptist clergyman from Chicago, as an institute for the training of young colored men for the Ministry, and continued to be used as such until about one year ago 1870, when, having received large accessions to their funds, the society bought a large building on Main street. This building was situated on the corner of Main and 19th streets, and was formerly known as the

UNITED STATES HOTEL.—It was built many years ago, and was at one time the leading hotel of the city, being at that time situated in the business portion of the city; but trade went up town, visitors fell off, and the house gradually became unpopular, until 1850, when it was closed altogether. It was put to various uses, until finally sold to trustees for the purpose to which it is now applied. It is being well fitted up as a school, with lodging and recitation rooms, and apartments for the principal and his assistants. About sixty young colored men are here under instruction, and some fifteen or twenty ministers are turned out each year. The institution is under charge of Rev. C. H. Corey, D. D.

THE COUNTY COURT HOUSE

Is situated at the corner of 22d and Main streets. There is nothing specially attractive about the building. But in the musty records of the clerk's office may be found some of the oldest deeds, wills, &c., to be met with in the State. Henrico county was one of the eight original shires of the State, as it was the most westerly, running back, if we are not misinformed, as far west as the Ohio, and possibly beyond. It has been divided and cut down until but little of its fair proportions remain; but the many old quaint and curious papers of this once widely extending county are kept here.

PUBLIC PARKS.

As yet the city authorities have not paid as much attention to these "lungs of the city" as they should, but in the Capitol Square Richmond has a park which would do honor to any city in the country. It is oblong, and contains about sixteen acres. It was originally very rough and rugged, but under the direction of Mons. Godefroi, and more recently under that of Mr. Notman, of Philadelphia, it has assumed its present beautiful and picturesque appearance. The grounds are adorned with the various kinds of forest trees indigenous to Virginia, besides linden and other exotic trees. Since the war many trees of American varieties have been brought and transplanted, some of them from the far west. Broad and shady walks wind through and around this park, and numbers of seats invite the weary pedestrian or pleasure-seeker to sit down in the shade of the trees. Two fountains, on opposite sides of the park, send up their cooling waters.

Monroe Park is in the western part of the city. It has only been recently laid out, and planted with trees and shrubbery. It has also been adorned with a bronze statue of Washington, by Hubard—an exact copy of Houdon's statue. in the Capitol building.

THE CITY SPRING PARK is a popular resort for nurses and their charges. It is entered from Seventh or Eighth streets. This park presents few attractions to strangers.

CEMETERIES.

HOLLYWOOD CEMETERY should be visited by all who come to Richmond, however short their stay may be. It may be reached either by the City Railway, whose terminus is just at the gate, or by carriage at city rates. It lies on the banks of the James River, south-west of the city, and comprises, including the recent additions in order to make room for the soldiers graves, over sixty acres. For beauty of natural scenery, Hollywood Cemetery can be surpassed by few in this country.

The soldiers' section occupies the greater part of an almost unshaded hill immediately at one gate and not far from the other. Here are interred the remains of five thousand Confederate soldiers, each grave being distinctly marked by a small numbered stone erected by the ladies of the Hollywood Memorial Association. The numbers on the stones refer to a Memorial Register issued by the Association, in which may be found the names of a large proportion of the soldiers here buried—some, of course, as in all large cemeteries, are unknown. The Register may be obtained of Mrs. E. H. Brown, Secretary of the Association.

The most conspicuous object in the cemetery from any avenue of approach, and the most intereresting to tourists generally is the Confederate Memorial Pile, erected by the ladies of the South in memory of the Southern dead. It is located on a high hill, and is ninety feet high and about forty feet square at the base.

The design is most unique. At present it seems to be a mere pyramid of unhewn granite blocks, piled up with little idea of forming a beautiful structure. But when the vines now showing themselves a few feet above the base shall have taken firm root and spread abroad their clinging branches until the whole pyramid is covered with verdure, the effect will be striking and picturesque. On the east side of the monument appears the inscription: "To the Confederate Dead;" on the north the motto: "*Memoria in Æterna*," and on the west the legend: "Erected by the Ladies of the Hollywood Memorial Association, A. D., 1869."

Once a year, on the day set apart for the decoration of the graves of the Confederate dead, when the beautiful cemetery is thronged with people from Richmond and the surrounding country, the apex of the pyramid, notwithstanding its giddy height, is invariably crowned with a wreath of laurel, by some venturesome youth. It is no easy task to accomplish this feat without the aid of a ladder, but it is always done.

The most notable graves in Hollywood are those of General J. E. B. Stuart, the great cavalry leader of the Southern Confederacy; Lieutenant General A. P. Hill, one of Lee's most trusted officers; General W. H. Stevens, Chief Engineer of the Army of Northern Virginia; General John Pegram, and his brother, the Colonel; and Captain O. Jennings Wise, son of Governor Henry A. Wise, and a celebrated editor of the Richmond *Enquirer*. Many Confederate officers, ranging in rank from General to subaltern, are interred in private lots. In one of the private vaults the remains of General John H. Morgan, the great Kentucky guerilla, were deposited for two or three years, until removed to his own beloved State.

The monument to Bishop Meade, one of the foremost churchmen of the country, a historian of the Old Dominion, and for many years Bishop of the Diocese of Virginia, was erected by the people of the diocese within the last few years. It bears a most affectionate and appropriate inscription.

Above the remains of Ex-President Monroe is reared an iron tomb, beautiful in design and perfect in workmanship. Monroe was buried in New York, but in 1857 his body was escorted to Richmond by the Seventh Regiment of New York Volunteers, and deposited on the brow of the hill in Hollywood now covered by this monument. The military and civic display attending the second interment was such as should be made at the death of one of the merits and high position of this son of Virginia.

About one mile east of the city, on a little eminence, gently sloping towards the rising sun, is OAKWOOD CEMETERY. These grounds, embracing some forty acres, were purchased by the city about fifteen years ago, and laid off in burial lots, comparatively few of which have been sold, persons preferring the more beautiful grounds of Hollywood. Nature has not done so much for the beautifying of this as her sister cemetery; but, far removed from the busy world around—no noisy hum of crowded mart, nor clattering wheel of mill disturbs the mourner here. All is quiet as the grave itself. The spot is sacred, too, in the eyes of all southerners, for here lie eighteen thousand of the sons of the South who fell fighting for what they believed to be right. Every Southern state is here represented, and here in the early spring the fair hands of Virginia ladies strew flowers over the graves of these heroes of the " Lost Cause."

The graves of the soldiers have each a head-board whereon is neatly painted the name of the dead, with his company, regiment and State, so far as the facts could be ascertained. The corner stone of a monument in memory of the Confederate dead was laid here in May 1871, and it was expected that the monument would be completed in a year from that time. The graves are carefully cared for by the ladies of the Oakwood Memorial Association, and the funds for building the monument were collected through the same instrumentality.

SHOCKOE HILL CEMETERY is located in the northern part of the city, in the neighborhood of the City Alms House. It has many fine tomb-stones and is a popular place of burial. Nearly all the graves are over-run with flowers and creeping vines. Just in rear of it is THE JEWISH CEMETERY, which is worth visiting. It is neatly enclosed and handsomely adorned. The graves of the Confederate soldiers (nearly all Hebrews,) are surrounded by an elegant and appropriate iron railing, cast to represent arms and ammunition.

THE NATIONAL CEMETERY is located on the Williamsburg road, about two miles from Richmond. The Federal Government has collected the bones of thousands of Union soldiers from the cemeteries and battle-fields of Virginia, and deposited them here, where a careful and loving watch may be kept over their graves by those for whom they fought. Money has been lavishly expended in making the place attractive, and that object has been accomplished. Every grave has been turfed, and each is marked by a neat white head-board, bearing, when possible, the name and antecedents of him who sleeps below. There are hundreds, however, whose names could not be ascertained, and one sees on all sides such inscriptions as " one unknown U. S. soldier," "two unknown U. S. soldiers," and sometimes " *four* unknown U. S. soldiers." The graves are always decorated on the 30th May, under the supervision of the Grand Army of the Republic.

FINE VIEWS.

There are views in and around our city, which, for beauty and variety of landscape, are unsurpassed in this State. That from the top of the Capitol building, forty feet above the highest surrounding buildings, is grand in the extreme. When the tourist emerges through the sky-light in the roof, the first view which meets his eyes is of Church and Union Hills, the most prominent object being St. John's Church, so deeply embowered in trees that only the steeple is visible. The other churches, taller than the houses around them, stand out in bold relief. Maddox Hill, Howard's Grove, the Central Lunatic Asylum—the once famous Fairfield Race Course, Oakwood Cemetery, Battery No. 5, and Mount Erin, are all in full view. As we turn to the right we see all the lower portion of the city, including Rocketts. The river, too, is here seen, stretching like molten silver far away, the eye distinctly marking its course until it is lost around the curve at Drewry's Bluff. With a good glass may be distinctly seen several old country seats, amongst them are " Wilton," " Cockamouth," " Chatsworth," " Tree Hill," " Powhatan" and " Marion Hill."

Turning still more to the right, the vision crosses the river and rests on Manchester; the once celebrated Falls Plantation—the hospitable residence of the Marx family, while around and through it, over extensive fields, are now seen neat little cottages, and well tilled patches of ground. Still turning, the vision is shortened by the hills of Chesterfield; but we see Mayo's, the Danville and Petersburg bridges, all of which span the river just here; and above them may be seen Belle Isle, with its large iron foundry, while the river leaping over the rocks with a roar often heard for miles, and running around and between them in many a whirl and eddy, and the numberless green islands which are presented to view, form together as picturesque a scene as the eye of the tourist ever rests upon. Turning further to the right, we see the Tredegar Works, the old State Armory, the Canal, Pump-House, Penitentiary, and last of all, Hollywood, that beautiful city of the dead, and popular resort of the living, with its spire of unhewn granite, raised in honor of the Confederate dead, lifting its peak above the tops of the tallest trees surrounding it. All around us is beauty and quiet, for at our great altitude from the ground no noise, save that of the everroaring falls, reaches us. We look down on the houses, the churches and the monuments.

Beautiful views may also be obtained from "Libby's" and "Gamble's" Hills. These spots are always visited by tourists, and many of our citizens find ever increasing gratification in the scenery, as day after day they visit these commanding heights to enjoy the delightful river breezes, which are always found here.

DOWN JAMES RIVER.

The ride down James River during the summer or

early fall, is one of the most delightful which can be taken by the tourist or pleasure-seeker. The gentle and easy curves of the stream, the cool and refreshing breezes, and the untiring courtesy and politeness of the officers of the river boats, all serve to make it a charming trip. As the steamer glides along there are to be seen large and finely cultivated plantations, houses whose date of erection is far back in the colonial times, ruins whose walls, could they speak, would tell us wondrous tales of the gay cavaliers, and high born ladies who once occupied them, and roamed over the extensive grounds surrounding them. But the day of their glory has passed.

Near these old residences may now be seen the low dirty hut of the negro, and on the broad bosom of the river where once floated the boats of the cavalier may now be seen the clumsy fishing boat and the winged messengers of commerce.

The site of the ancient town of WARWICK, a few miles south of the city, is pointed out to the traveler, but nought of the town remains, save the old grave yard and broken wharf. Lower down are still seen standing a portion of the earth works of FORT DARLING, built to resist the invasion of Tarleton, during the revolutionary war. Still further on we see the extensive works of DREWRY'S BLUFF, erected during the late war. A mile beyond, on the opposite side of the river, is CHAFFIN'S BLUFF, a fortification scarcely less formidable than the other. Just below this point is DUTCH GAP CANAL, then VARINA, where the exchange of prisoners took place; and DEEP BOTTOM, where the iron clad fleet protected the army of General McClellan, after the battle of MALVERN HILL. Further down is the spot known for nearly two centuries as Bermuda Hundreds, and then we reach City Point, where General Grant received the supplies for his army, when he invested Petersburg. There are numerous other places of note, but none of importance until the steamer touches at JAMESTOWN. These ruins are to the Southerner, what Plymouth Rock is to the New Englander, for here the first settlement in British America was made by Captain John Smith, on the 13th May, 1607. The site is a point of land projecting into the James. Little now remains of the first settlement, except the ivy-covered tower of the church, where worshipped Smith and his fellow-colonists. It is not known positively when the church to which this tower belonged was built, but it is supposed that the ruins are nearly two hundred and fifty years old. Leaving the boat at Jamestown, the tourist may by a drive reach

WILLIAMSBURG, the seat of Government for the State of Virginia from 1698 to 1779. Here are at present located William and Mary College and the Eastern Lunatic Asylum. But the scope of this work does not admit of a description of the many interesting relics to be found at these places, nor of a further account of the ride down the James. The tourist is now far beyond Richmond. Suffice it to say that much of interest may be seen on either side of the river even down to its mouth, where NEWPORT'S NEWS presents itself, its harbor memorable as the scene of the burning of the CONGRESS and sinking of the CUMBERLAND in the MERRIMAC fight of 1862.

PLEASANT DRIVES.

THERE are six principal roads leading into the city from the surrounding country. Commencing at the river on the east, we have, first, the Osborne turnpike—turnpike no longer, for the toll-gates have long since been taken down. This road a mile below the city runs by POWHATAN—once the seat of King Powhatan, and the scene of the intervention of Pocahontas to save Captain John Smith—and Chaffin's Farm, on which the fortifications of "CHAFFIN'S BLUFF" were erected. Branching off from this road at Tree Hill is the New Market or Varina road, leading to Charles City Court House. This is the direct route to FORT HARRISON, VARINA, DUTCH GAP, MALVERN HILL, HARRISON'S LANDING, and other places of note during the war.

WILLIAMSBURG ROAD.—Entering the city at the same point is the Williamsburg road, which branches about one and a half miles below the city, one fork leading through Darbytown, on by Fussell's Mill. The other passes the NATIONAL CEMETERY near this city, and at Seven Pines running near the celebrated battle fields of SAVAGE'S STATION and SEVEN PINES, or "FAIR OAKS," to New Kent Court House.

NINE MILE ROAD.—Entering the city by way of Venable Street, (Union Hill) is the Nine Mile road, a highway which acquired much notoriety during the late war. It is also one of the drives to the field of SEVEN PINES.

MECHANICSVILLE TURNPIKE.—Directly from the eastern portion of the city, and entering it also by way of Venable and Eighteenth streets, is the Mechanicsville turnpike, a road leading to some of the most sanguinary and hotly contested battle fields of the war. ELLERSON'S MILL, GAINES' MILL, COLD HARBOR, and the scene of many a smaller fight and innumerable skirmishes, are reached by this drive.

THE MEADOW BRIDGE ROAD—Coming into the city on

Seventeenth street, affords a very pretty drive. A number of beautiful villas and well cultivated farms meet the eye of the traveler, and relieve the monotony of the landscapes, but it is chiefly interesting to tourists as the route by which Lieutenant General A. P. Hill led his corps to flank the army of McClellan—the commencement of the "seven days" fight. The *Meadow Bridge* over the Chickahominy is the spot where the first gun was fired in that memorable conflict.

THE BROOK TURNPIKE—Entering the city at its north-eastern corner, is another beautiful drive. Along this road are elegant houses, pretty cottages, and many truck or market gardens. Dahlgreen's nearest approach to the city, in his memorable raid in 1864, was on this road. On this occasion he approached within about a mile of the corporate limits.

DEEP RUN TURNPIKE, entering the city on Broad street, in former days received its support as a pike mainly by the many coal carts which brought coal from the *Deep Run Pits*, ten miles above the city. These pits are not now worked, but many a sunken shaft, half-filled, and many a pile of slate and black rock, give evidence of the busy scenes once witnessed in the now silent woods. An attempt was made a few years since to renew the working of these pits, but the enterprise failed, and they have been again abandoned. This road, about twelve miles from Richmond, falls into the

THREE CHOP ROAD, once one of the most famous in the State, inasmuch as it was the most direct route to Louisville, Kentucky. By this highway the droves of horses, mules and cattle from that prolific country were driven to the eastern markets. It is now used mostly for neighborhood purposes, and the road-side taverns which once gave nightly " entertainment for man and beast" are no more. This, as well as other roads in this portion of the State, bears the marks made by the hogsheads of tobacco, when it was the practice to *roll* them to market, by passing a pole through the middle and fastening thereto a pair of shafts, to which a horse was attached. The *holes* made by the rolling hogsheads, each one taking up a portion of mud and depositing it further on, are still seen, though more than a half century has elapsed since this mode of transportation has been abandoned.

THE GROVE ROAD affords a short and pleasant evening drive. It is reached by Grace or Franklin streets, and runs from the latter up through Sidney, uniting with the Deep Run Turnpike about two miles from the city. On this road, many of our merchants and other business men have bought land and built modern residences. There is no more fashionable drive than out Franklin street.

THE WESTHAM ROAD enters the extreme western part of the city. It passes through the most improving suburbs, and in full view of Hollywood Cemetery, the Reservoir and Camp Grant, or Harvie, goes by some of the finest farms on the upper James River, and leads to the ancient town of Westham.

THE WAY TO THE BATTLE-FIELDS AROUND RICHMOND.

COLD HARBOR—Seven miles from Richmond, is reached by the Mechanicsville road.

SEVEN PINES or Fair Oaks, about nine miles from Richmond, is reached by the Williamsburg road ; and
C

the York River Railroad passes through the battle-field.

Savage's Station is reached by the same lines of travel as Seven Pines.

Ellerson's Mill, about six miles from the city, is reached by the Mechanicsville road.

Fort Harrison is near the Osborne Pike or River road, and is about eleven miles from Richmond.

Malvern Hill, about fifteen miles distant, is most accessible by the River and New Market roads.

Deep Bottom and Varina are reached by the same roads.

Gaines' Mill, just below Ellerson's, is, like that battle-field, reached by the Mechanicsville road.

Atlee's is on the Chesapeake and Ohio Railroad, about nine miles from Richmond; and Hanover Court House is on the same road and about seventeen miles from the city.

A description of the battles is beyond the province of this little work—nor can we pretend to catalogue the numerous localities in which skirmishes were fought.

Further reference to the battle-fields may be found under the caption—"Pleasant Drives."

THE MARSHALL HOUSE.

At the south-west corner of Marshall and Ninth streets, stands an unpretending two-story brick building, built by Chief Justice Marshall about 1795, and in which he resided until his death in 1835. The property has ever since remained in the family, being now owned by his grand daughter Miss Mary Harvie. It is at present occupied by Ex-Governor Henry A. Wise, late General in the C. S. A.

ST. JOHN'S CHURCH.

[From "Walks about Richmond"]

CITY CHURCHES.

CATHOLIC.—St. Peter's Cathedral, corner Grace and Eighth streets, Right Rev. John McGill, D. D., Bishop of the Diocese.

St Patrick's, Twenty-fifth street, between Broad and Grace.

St. Mary's (German), Marshall, between Third and Fourth streets.

EPISCOPAL.—St. Paul's, corner Grace and Ninth streets.

Monumental, Broad, between Twelfth and Thirteenth streets.

Grace, corner Main and Foushee streets.

St. James, Fifth street, corner of Marshall.

St. John's, Broad, corner Twenty-fifth street.

St. Mark's, Fourth street, between Clay and Leigh.

PRESBYTERIAN.—First Church, corner of Tenth and Capitol streets.

Second, Fifth street, between Main and Franklin.

Third, corner Twenty-fifth and Broad Streets.

Grace-street (formerly the United,) corner of Grace and Fourth streets.

CHURCH OF THE DISCIPLES.—Sycamore, meets temporarily at Universalist Church, on Mayo street.

BAPTIST.—First Church, corner Broad and Twelfth streets.

Second, Main corner of Sixth street.

Grace Street, corner of Foushee and Grace streets.

Leigh-street, Leigh, corner Twenty fifth street, Church Hill.

Pine-street—Oregon Hill.

Fulton, Rocketts.

Sidney, Sidney.

LUTHERAN.—St. John's (German), Fifth street, between Leigh and Jackson.

Bethlehem (Evangelical,) Sixth street, near Clay.

FRIENDS MEETING-HOUSE, Clay street, between First and Foushee.

METHODIST EPISCOPAL.—Broad-Street, corner Broad and Tenth streets.

Centenary, Grace, between Fourth and Fifth streets.

Clay street, corner of Adams and Clay.

Trinity, corner of Broad and 20th streets.

Union Station, Union Hill.

There are churches also in Sidney, Oregon Hill and Rocketts.

JEWISH.—Congregation House of Israel, synagogue, Broad, between Ninth and Tenth streets.

Bayth Ahabah, Eleventh street, near Clay.

Kenneseth Israel, Mayo street, between Broad and Ross.

Beth Shalom, Mayo street, between Broad and Ross.

COLORED CHURCHES.—The most noted colored church is the First African, (Baptist) on Broad and College streets. This church is said to have the largest membership of any church in the world.

Chimborazo, (Baptist) on Chimborazo Hill is a popular place of worship.

Second Church (Baptist,) near the Penitentiary.

There is also a methodist church on Third street, near the Poor House with a large membership. All these churches have colored pastors, whose ministrations appear to give entire satisfaction to the congregations.

CHARITABLE INSTITUTIONS.

St. Joseph's Orphan Asylum, corner of Marshall and

Fourth streets, was founded by Father O'Brien in 1835. There are three departments of the institution—the asylum proper, the academy, and the parochial school on Fourth street. The asylum numbers sixty-five beneficiaries, and the parochial school one hundred and twenty-five. The institution is under the management of Sister Mariana and thirteen other Sisters of Charity.

The Female Orphan Asylum was instituted about 1807. It is located on the corner of Leigh and Seventh streets, in a building erected through the liberality of the late Edmund Walls. It has at present but thirty-six beneficiaries, though it is capable of accommodating over one hundred. The officers are Mrs. L. M. Norton, president; Mrs. Wm. H. Macfarland, vice-president; Mrs. John L. Bacon, treasurer; Mrs. Dr. Peterfield Trent, secretary; Mrs. C. Gennett and others, directors.

The Male Orphan Asylum, located at Harvie, (formerly Camp Grant,) was founded in 1846. There are thirty-five boys in the asylum under the superintendence of Mr. Joseph W. Gill and his lady. Dr. W. W. Parker, president; A. T. Harris, W. K. Watts, Thomas D. Quarles, Wm. F. Taylor, vice-presidents; James Dunlop, treasurer; Charles U. Williams, Secretary; Dr. W. H. Gwathmey and others, directors.

PUBLIC BUILDINGS.

City Hall, corner of Broad, Capitol and Eleventh streets. In this building are the rooms of the Chancery and Hustings Courts, the offices of the Mayor, Collector of City Taxes, Commissioner of the Revenue, Auditor, City Engineer, Clerk of the Council, Inspector of Gas, City Sergeant, Sealer of Weights and Measures, and the Council Chamber and Jury Rooms.

City Jail, corner Marshall street and Jail alley.

Alms House, at the northern extermity of Third street. This is a splendid and commodious building—admirably kept.

State Penitentiary, on Oregon Hill, within the corporate limits.

County Court House and Jail, corner of Main and Twenty-second streets.

State Court House, Eleventh street, between Broad and Marshall.

First Market, Main street, corner Seventeenth, running back to Grace street.

Second Market, corner of Broad and Sixth streets.

Police Headquarters and First Police Station, over the First Market, corner Main and Seventeenth streets.

Second Police Station, over Second Market, corner Sixth and Broad streets.

Third Police Station, over Engine House, on Brook Avenue.

Circuit Court Rooms, Stearns' building, opposite Post Office.

Assembly Hall, Eighth between Franklin and Grace streets.

Washington Hall, Broad, between Ninth and Tenth streets.

St. Alban's Hall, corner Third and Main streets.

Masons' Hall, Franklin street, between Eighteenth and Nineteenth.

Pythian Hall, corner of Eleventh and Bank streets.

Marshall Hall, corner of Tenth and Bank streets.

Odd Fellows' Hall, corner of Franklin and Mayo streets.

SPRINGFIELD HALL, corner Twenty-sixth and M streets

CITY WATER WORKS OFFICE, under Washington Hall, Broad between Ninth and Tenth streets.

CORN AND FLOUR EXCHANGE, corner Cary and Twelfth streets.

TOBACCO EXCHANGE, Thirteenth street, near Cary.

CHAMBER OF COMMERCE ROOMS, over First National Bank of Richmond, Main street, between Eleventh and Twelfth.

YOUNG MEN'S CHRISTIAN ASSOCIATION ROOMS, under Pythian Hall, corner of Eleventh and Main streets.

CENTRAL LUNATIC ASYLUM for the colored insane, Howard's Grove.

TOBACCO WAREHOUSES.

Either of these will be found worth visiting by those unacquainted with the handling of tobacco. The principal ones are the SHOCKOE on Shockoe Slip, south of Cary street; the PUBLIC on the south-side of the Basin; MAYO'S between the river and the Dock near Mayo's Bridge; and SEABROOK'S, on Grace, between Seventeenth and Eighteenth streets.

RAILROAD DEPOTS.

RICHMOND, FREDERICKSBURG AND POTOMAC, corner of Eighth and Byrd streets, and Broad street corner of Eighth.

RICHMOND AND DANVILLE, near the river between Thirteenth and Fourteenth streets.

RICHMOND AND YORK RIVER, Cary street, between Twenty-Fourth and Twenty-Fifth.

RICHMOND AND PETERSBURG, corner of Eighth and Byrd streets.

CHESAPEAKE AND OHIO, corner Broad and Seventeenth streets.

NEWSPAPER OFFICES.

DAILY, SEMI-WEEKLY AND WEEKLY DISPATCH, by Cowardin & Ellyson, corner Twelfth and Main streets.

DAILY, SEMI WEEKLY AND WEEKLY ENQUIRER, by Enquirer Publishing Company, Main, between Twelfth and Thirteenth streets.

DAILY, SEMI-WEEKLY AND WEEKLY WHIG, by J. C. Shields, corner of Franklin and Governor streets.

DAILY, SEMI-WEEKLY AND WEEKLY STATE JOURNAL, by J. T. Daniels, Main, between Ninth and Tenth streets.

EVENING NEWS, by W. H. Wade & Co., Ninth between Main & Franklin.

VIRGINIA GAZETTE, (German daily,) by Gazette Publishing Co., Main, between Seventh and Eighth streets.

RICHMOND ANZEIGER, (German daily), by B. Hassel, Governor, between Main and Franklin streets.

SECRET BENEVOLENT ORDERS.

MASONIC.—Richmond Lodge, No. 10, meets at Masons' Hall, on Franklin street, on the first Tuesday in each month.

Richmond Randolph Lodge, No. 19, meets at Masons' Hall, on Franklin street, on the third Tuesday in each month.

Metropolitan Lodge, No. 11, meets at St. Albans Hall, corner of Third and Main streets, on the second Thursday in each month.

Loge Francais, No. 53, meets at Washington Hall. on Broad street, on the second Monday of each month.

St. John's Lodge, No. 36, meets at Washington Hall, on Broad street, on the second Tuesday of each month.

Joppa Lodge, No. 40, meets at St. Albans corner of Third and Main streets, on the Fourth Thursday of each month.

Dove Lodge, No. 51, meets at Washington Hall, on Broad street, on the Fourth Friday in each month.

Temple Lodge, No. 9, meets at St. Albans Hall, corner Third and Main streets, on the first Friday of each month.

Henrico Union Lodge, No. 130, meets at Masonic Hall, Twenty-fifth street, on the first Monday of each month.

Richmond Royal Arch Chapter, No. 3, meets at Masons' Hall, on Franklin street, on the first Thursday, in each month.

Lafayette Royal Arch Chapter, No. 43, meets at Washington Hall, on Broad street, on the Third Thursday in each month.

St. Albans Royal Arch Chapter, No. 33, meets at St. Alban's Hall, corner Third and Main streets, on the first Monday in each month.

Harman Royal Arch Chapter, No. 53, meets at Masonic Hall, on Twenty-fifth street, on the third Monday of each month.

Richmond Commandery, No. 2, Knights Templar, meets at the Asylum on Franklin street, between Eighteenth and Nineteenth, on the fourth Tuesday of each month.

INDEPENDENT ORDER ODD FELLOWS.—Jefferson Lodge, No. 4, meets every Monday night at Odd Fellows' Hall, corner of Franklin and Mayo streets.

Union, No. 7, meets at Odd Fellows' Hall every Friday night.

Friendship, No. 10, meets every Tuesday night at Odd Fellows' Hall.

Powhatan No. 12, meets on Wednesday nights at Odd Fellows' Hall.

Fitzhugh, No. 93, meets every Tuesday night at Fitzhugh Hall, Broad street near Sixth.

Aurora, No. 116, meets at the hall, corner of Second and Broad streets every Wednesday evening.

Schiller, No. 139, Sixth and Marshall streets, every Wednesday evening.

Roane, No. 130, meets every Saturday night, at the Masonic Hall, on Twenty-fifth street.

Henderson, No. 105, meets in hall over engine house, Manchester, every Monday night.

Stewart, No. 141, meets every Tuesday night, in Manchester.

Neilson Encampment No. 2, meets on the First and Third Thursdays of each month, at Odd Fellows' Hall.

Excelsior Encampment, No. 22, meets at Odd Fellows's Hall, on the Second and Fourth Thursdays of each month.

Grand Lodge, of Virginia, I. O. O. F., meets annually in the city of Richmond on the Wednesday after the second Monday in April, at Odd Fellows' Hall.

Grand Encampment of Virginia meets at Odd Fellows's Hall, immediately after the adjournment of the Grand Lodge.

RED MEN.—Pocahontas Tribe, No. 14, I. O. R. M., meets at Marshall Hall, corner Bank and Eleventh streets, every Wednesday evening.

Chickahominy Tribe, No. 34, I. O. R. M., meets at Springfield Hall, corner Twenty-sixth and M streets, every Tuesday night.

Annawan, No. 34, I. O. R. M., meets at Marshall Hall, corner Eleventh and Bank streets, every Monday evening.

Sycamore, No. 91, I. O. R. M., meets at Blenner's Hall, corner Sixth and Marshall streets, every Thursday evening.

INDEPENDENT ORDER B'NAI B'RITH.—Rimmon Lodge, No. 68, meets on the first and third Sundays of each month at Covenant Hall, on Capitol Street.

Benjamin, No. 69, meets on the second and fourth Sundays of each month at Covenant Hall.

SONS OF TEMPERANCE.—Springfield Division, No. 167, meets at Springfield Hall, corner Twenty-sixth and M streets, every Thursday night.

Shockoe Hill, No. 54, meets at Covenant Hall, on Capitol street, every Friday night.

Marion, No. 5, meets in the Sunday School Room of the Sidney M. E. Church, every Tuesday night.

Fidelity, No. 44, meets at Fitzhugh Hall, Broad street, every Thursday night.

West End, No. 7, meets at Jackson Hall, corner of Second and Broad streets, every Tuesday night.

FRIENDS OF TEMPERANCE.—Stonewall Council, No. 74, meets at Springfield Hall, every Monday night.

Manchester Council, No. 102, meets at Town Hall, Manchester, every Tuesday night.

TEMPLARS OF HONOR AND TEMPERANCE.—Undine Temple, No. 2, meets in Covenant Hall, on the first, third, and fifth Thursday evenings of each month.

St. John's Degree Council, meets in Covenant Hall, on the second and and fourth Thursday evenings of each month.

Old Dominion Section No. 1, Independent Order

Cadets of Honor and Temperance, meets every Monday evening in Fitzhugh Hall, corner Sixth and Broad streets.

KNIGHTS OF PYTHIAS.—Virginia Lodge, No. 2, meets at Pythian Hall, corner Eleventh and Main streets, every Monday night.

Old Dominion, No. 4, meets at Pythian Hall, corner Eleventh and Main streets, every Tuesday night.

Syracuse, No. 5, meets at Marshall Hall, corner Tenth and Bank streets, every Friday night.

Damon, No. 7, meets at Masons' Hall, on Twenty-fifth street, every Friday night.

Marshall, No. 12, meets at Jackson Hall, corner Second and Broad streets, every Thursday night.

Richmond, No. 14, meets at Pythian Hall, corner Eleventh and Main streets, every Thursday night.

Germania No. 15, meets at Marshall Hall, corner Tenth and Bank streets, every Thursday night.

Hines, No. 17, meets at Pythian Hall, corner Eleventh and Main streets, every Friday night.

Jefferson, No. 23, meets at Odd Fellows' Hall, corner Franklin and Mayo streets, every Wednesday night.

Myrtle, No. 25, just instituted at date of this publication.

TOWN OF MANCHESTER.

MANCHESTER lies immediately opposite Richmond, and contains about two thousand five hundred inhabitants. It is situated on ground gently rising from the river, which gives it a very picturesque appearance as viewed from this side.

It has several churches, and the society is as good as in any other portion of the State. It is celebrated for its water power and its manufactories, having several

flouring mills, an iron foundry, several cotton factories, &c., &c., all in successful operation. There
are many beautiful houses in the town, and it was once
a favorite residence of our merchants. Its population
is steadily on the increase, and its suburbs may at no
distant day again become a popular retreat for our city
business men.

There are several very fine drives leading out of
Manchester—one to the *Midlothian Coal Pits,* distant
about eleven miles; and another takes the traveler to *the
ruins of Bellona Arsenal,* on James River, twelve miles
off. This Arsenal, formerly a depot for United States
Military stores, was founded in 1816, and attached to it
was one of the oldest cannon foundries in the Union.
Some of the best guns used in this country in *ante bel-
lum* days were cast at this foundry, and mounted on the
ramparts of Fortress Monroe. During the war it was
revived, and many pieces of ordinance were turned
out from its works for the use of the Confederates.
After the evacuation, however, it was not used, and a
few years ago it was fired by an incendiary and entirely
consumed.

Another road runs off in the direction of Petersburg,
and over this, in former years, all the travel between
the two cities passed. It passes through the village of
Chester, and very near the now historic localities of
Drewry's Bluff and Fort Darling.

LEGAL CHARGES FOR CARS AND HACKS.

ALL visitors to the city are advised to examine carefully the following legal charges for hack-hire, baggage
transportation and street car fare. These charges are
established by the city ordinances, and should a driver

persist in making an illegal demand, he should be reported to a policeman, that the law in such case, made
and provided, may be enforced.

For carrying a person in a hack not more
    than ten squares,   ·   ·   ·   50 cts.
For each additional square, ·   ·   5 cts.

Provided that the whole charge for carrying one person
to any part of the city, shall not exceed $1.00.

The charge for carrying not more than four persons
shall not for the whole, exceed $1.50; unless more
than one hour be employed, and then for the first hour
only $1.50, and for each succeeding hour, 50 cents. No
charge shall be made for children under three years of
age.

For carrying persons between ten o'clock at night
and day break, an additional charge of one-half the
above rates, and no more, may be made.

For baggage, the charge shall be for each trunk carried outside, 25 cents; and nothing shall be charged
for any article carried inside, or for any carpet bag or
basket in hand.

On the City Railway the fare is 10 cents for an
adult, or 5 cents for a child under five years of age—
Three tickets, however may be bought for a quarter
or twelve for one dollar.

☞ Sixteen squares are counted as one mile.

STEREOSCOPIC AND CARD VIEWS

of

RICHMOND AND VICINITY.

Published and for sale by

SELDEN & CO.,

Dealers in

Photograph and Stereoscopic Views, Stereoscopes, Photograph Albums, Cartes de Visite, Stationery, Plain and Ornamental Frames, Passe par Touts, Confederate Currency, Curiosities, &c., &c.

No. 918 Main Street, (3d door from cor. 10th,)

RICHMOND, VA.

Catalogues furnished on application.

The Richmond, Fredericksburg & Potomac

RAILROAD

FORMS AN IMPORTANT LINK IN THE

Great Through Line between the North and South.

COMING SOUTH Passengers leave the wharf of the Potomac Steamers at the time named in the schedule of the day, and enjoy a delightful trip down the river, passing in full view of many places of historic note including

MOUNT VERNON—THE HOME OF WASHINGTON.

At Acquia creek connection is made with the cars which make quick time to Richmond, running through FREDERICKSBURG, HAMILTON'S CROSSING, ASHLAND AND HANOVER JUNCTION, and by several famous battle-fields, including

MARYE'S HEIGHTS.

GOING NORTH Passengers leave the depot, corner of Byrd and Eighth streets, Richmond, on schedule time, and the trip is equally agreeable.

☞ NIGHT TRAINS are supplied with comfortable sleeping chairs and NIGHT BOATS with comfortable State Rooms and Berths. No efforts are spared to make this

OLD AND FAVORITE ROUTE

Continue the most attractive.

☞ THROUGH TICKETS & THROUGH BAGGAGE CHECKED TO ALL POINTS NORTH, SOUTH, EAST AND WEST.

J. B. GENTRY,
Gen'l Ticket Ag't.

E. D. T. MYERS,
Gen'l Superintendent.

RICHMOND & PETERSBURG R. R.

This popular line of travel affords

THE SHORTEST AND MOST DIRECT CONNECTION

Between the roads going northward from Richmond, and southward from Weldon, N. C.

SMOOTH ROAD,

GOOD CARS,

FAST TIME.

Connection made at Petersburg with the Weldon Railroad, with the Atlantic, Mississippi and Ohio Railroad, for Lynchburg, Bristol and the South-west, with the same road to Norfolk and with the branch road to City Point, on James River.

TOURISTS should not fail to visit

THE BATTLE-FIELDS ABOUT PETERSBURG,

The scenes of some of the most celebrated fights during the civil war.   That city is only twenty-two miles distant from Richmond.

☞ For schedule see daily papers.

THOS. H. WYNNE,
President.

R. B. KASEY,
Ticket & Freight Ag't

New & Popular Route to New York

BY

LAND AND WATER.

Tourists desiring to take the most delightful route from Richmond to **Norfolk, Philadelphia, Baltimore,** or **New York,** should go

Down the James River

On the splendid steamer John Sylvester to Norfolk, thence by the

BAY LINE TO BALTIMORE.

The trip down the historic James, in the day-time, is one of the most agreeable to tourists that can be imagined. The scenery is beautiful, and the boat passes in full of

Drewry's Bluff, Fort Darling, Chaffin's Bluff, Varina, Dutch Gap Canal, Howlett's, Bermuda Hundreds, City Point, Jamestown,

And other places of note during the war.

Fare Excellent—Accommodations First-Class.

☞ For time of arrival and departure of Steamer, see Richmond papers of the day.

BAGGAGE CHECKED THROUGH.

L. B. TATUM,
Gen'l Ag't James River Steamboat Co.

THROUGH LINE FROM

NEW YORK TO NEW ORLEANS.

THE RICHMOND AND DANVILLE R. R.

On this favorite route from Richmond to Greensboro' will be found a road of easy grades and comfortable cars. The time made is as quick as that made on any southern railroad.

Passengers are received from the Richmond, Fredericksburg and Potomac Railroad in Richmond without change of cars.

CLOSE CONNECTIONS

Are made at Greensboro' with the North Carolina Central Railroad.

Tourists taking this route pass through the GREAT WHEAT AND TOBACCO GROWING REGION OF VIRGINIA, and see some phases of southern life to be seen nowhere else.

TWO FAST TRAINS DAILY,

(Except Sunday,) when there is only one. The through Mail, Express and Passenger train makes close connection with trains arriving from the north.

THROUGH TICKETS

To all points South and West can be procured at the ticket office in Richmond.

T. M. R. TALCOTT,

Eng'r and Sup't.

JNO. R. MACMURDO,

Gen'l Frg't & Ticket Ag't.

Real Estate Trust Company,

No. 1014 Main St., Richmond

AUTHORIZED CAPITAL, - - $200,000.

PAYS SEVEN PER CENT. ON DEPOSITS.

Offers its services to the public, and is prepared to do business as a

SAVINGS BANK.

Sums of **ONE DOLLAR** and upwards received on deposit, and **SEVEN PER CENT**. interest allowed on same.

Offers undoubted security, as it invests its funds in real estate securities.

To Capitalists seeking **INVESTMENT**, and Immigrants wishing to buy **REAL ESTATE** this company offers great attractions.

A. Q. HOLLADAY,
PRESIDENT.

E. B. NEWBURN,
SECRETARY.

WALKS ABOUT RICHMOND.

www.ingramcontent.com/pod-product-compliance
Lightning Source LLC
Chambersburg PA
CBHW021521090426
42739CB00007B/717